CANADA'S PRAIRIE ANIMALS

Chelsea Donaldson

Scholastic Canada Ltd.

Toronto New York London Auckland Sydney
Mexico City New Delhi Hong Kong Buenos Aires

Every reasonable effort has been made to trace the ownership of copyright material used in the text. The publisher would be pleased to know of any errors or omissions.

Visual Credits
Front cover: © Daniel J. Cox; pp. i (border), iii (border): Photodisc via SODA; pp. i (main image), 5, 15, 29, 33: © Roberta Olenick/Never-Spook-the-Animals Wildlife Photography; p. iv (map): HotHouse; pp. iv–1 (prairie scene): © Walter Bibikow/age fotostock/Maxx Images Inc.; p. 2: © Wayne Shiels/Lone Pine Photo; p. 3: © Tannis Shiels/Lone Pine Photo; p. 6: © Thomas Kitchin & Victoria Hurst; p. 7: © Don Johnston/age fotostock/Maxx Images Inc.; pp. 8–9: © Fritz Poelking/age footstock/Maxx Images Inc.; p. 10: © SuperStock/Maxx Images Inc.; pp. 11–12: Alan & Sandy Carey/Ivy Images; p. 13: © Lynn Stone/Animals Animals–Earth Scenes/Maxx Images Inc.; p. 14: © Charles Volkland/age fotostock/Maxx Images Inc.; pp. 16, 40–41: Jim Brandenburg/Minden Pictures; p. 17: © Gerlach Nature Photography/Animals Animals–Earth Scenes/Maxx Images Inc.; pp. 18–19: © Erwin & Peggy Bauer/Animals Animals–Earth Scenes/Maxx Images Inc.; p. 20: Daybreak Imagery/Animals Animals–Earth Scenes/Maxx Images Inc.; pp. 21, 42: © Tom & Pat Leeson; pp. 22–25: © Allen Blake Sheldon; p. 26: © Phyllis Greenberg/Animals Animals–Earth Scenes/Maxx Images Inc.; p. 27 (top r.): © E.A. Janes/age fotostock/Maxx Images Inc.; p. 27 (bottom l.): © John W. Warden/age fotostock/Maxx Images Inc.; p. 28: © McDonald Wildlife Photography/Animals Animals–Earth Scenes/Maxx Images Inc.; pp. 30, 38: Wayne Lankinen/Ivy Images; p. 32: © Victoria McCormick/Animals Animals–Earth Scenes/Maxx Images Inc.; p. 34: © Brian Milne/Animals Animals–Earth Scenes/Maxx Images Inc.; p. 35: © C.W. Schwartz/Animals Animals–Earth Scenes/Maxx Images Inc.; p. 36: © Leonard Rue Enterprises/Animals Animals–Earth Scenes/Maxx Images Inc.; p. 39: © Dominique Braud/Animals Animals–Earth Scenes/Maxx Images Inc.; p. 43: © Donald Higgs/Index Stock/Maxx Images Inc.; p. 44 (top): Allen Montgomery/U.S. Fish & Wildlife Service; p. 44 (bottom l.): U.S. Fish & Wildlife Service; p. 44 (bottom r.): James C. Leupold/U.S. Fish & Wildlife Service; back cover: Yellowstone National Park via SODA

Developed and Produced by Focus Strategic Communications Inc.
Project Management and Editorial: Adrianna Edwards
Design and Layout: Lisa Platt
Photo Research: Elizabeth Kelly

Special thanks to Dr. Bill Freedman of Dalhousie University for his expertise.

Library and Archives Canada Cataloguing in Publication
Donaldson, Chelsea, 1959-
Canada's prairie animals / Chelsea Donaldson.
(Canada close up)
ISBN-13 978-0-439-93666-8
ISBN-10 0-439-93666-7
1. Prairie animals—Canada—Juvenile literature.
I. Title. II. Series: Canada close up (Toronto, Ont.)
QL115.3.D65 2007   j591.74'0971   C2007-904656-5

10 9 8 7   Printed in Singapore   46   12 13 14 15

TABLE OF CONTENTS

Canada's Prairies

North Pole

Alaska

Canada

United States

Canadian Prairie Region
Canada
United States

Welcome to the Prairies!

Canada's prairies spread across southern Manitoba, Saskatchewan and Alberta. Thousands of years ago, thick ice covered this region. Then the ice melted. As the water drained away and dried up, it left a wide stretch of flat land. Many kinds of plants began to grow here.

The prairies have changed a lot since then. Farmers discovered that the soil was excellent for farming. Today, most of the land is used for growing grains and raising cattle.

The wild animals that lived here had to adapt to the changing land. Some, like the bison and the pronghorn, almost died out. Others have done very well in their new environment. Let's learn more about these prairie animals!

CHAPTER ONE

Richardson's Ground Squirrel

It's a calm day on the prairie. In an open field, a butterfly flits past. Flies buzz. Bumblebees dance from flower to flower. Mice creep through the short grass.

Suddenly, a furry creature pops up from a hole in the ground. It stands straight and still on its hind legs. Its alert eyes look into the distance for signs of danger. Then it drops down on all fours and begins its search for food.

For such a small creature, this animal has a lot of names. Some people call it a gopher or a prairie dog (but real gophers are much smaller, and prairie dogs are generally larger). Others call it a picketpin because it stands up so straight that it looks like a post on a picket fence. Still others call it a flickertail because that is how it communicates danger.

Its real name is Richardson's ground squirrel.

Whatever you call it, one thing is for sure: if you find one ground squirrel hole, there will be more nearby. They all lead to an amazing underground network of tunnels and chambers. There is even a toilet area. The whole burrow can be up to 10 metres long!

The burrows are big because the squirrels spend most of their lives underground. Some start their winter hibernation as early as mid-June. In spring and summer they come out only during the day. If it rains or is too hot, they go back underground.

Ground squirrels can be a nuisance to farmers. They eat new crops and grasses meant for cattle. They dig up newly planted fields. Horses can get hurt stepping in the holes that the squirrels leave behind.

But ground squirrels play an important role. Their burrows provide shelter to mice, voles and burrowing owls.
And hawks, badgers, weasels and foxes depend on ground squirrels for food.
Every creature has its place in nature.

CHAPTER TWO

Monarch Butterfly

Have you ever wondered why monarch butterflies are so brightly coloured? After all, those bright orange and black markings must make it easy for predators to spot them.

The reason for monarchs' fancy dress is to warn animals that they are not safe snacks. In fact, to most animals, monarchs are poisonous!

Monarchs get their poison from the milkweed plant. These plants are the only thing that monarch caterpillars eat. Later, when the caterpillars change into butterflies, they return to the milkweed to lay their eggs. Without milkweed, monarchs can't survive.

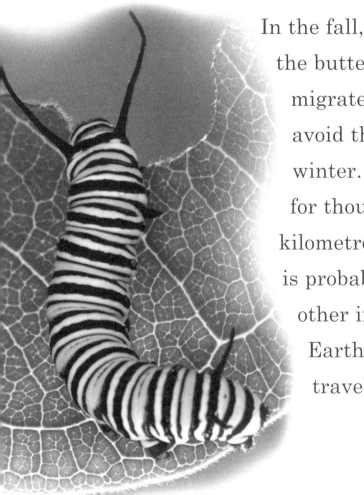

In the fall, the butterflies migrate south to avoid the harsh winter. They fly for thousands of kilometres. There is probably no other insect on Earth that travels as far.

For a long time, scientists couldn't figure out where the monarchs went. Then a team led by a Canadian scientist found out.

They tracked the butterflies to an area high in the mountains of Mexico. The trees in this area looked like they were covered with dead leaves. The branches seemed to be bending under the weight of their leaves.

But when the researchers looked closer, they saw the "leaves" were really millions of monarchs with folded wings. When the temperature rose, all the butterflies woke up and flew off at the same time.

The warmer weather must have told them it was time to return to the prairies!

CHAPTER THREE

Badger

The badger gets its name from the two black patches, or badges, on its cheeks. It has a broad flat forehead and a narrow snout. Its head is shaped like a pointed garden shovel.

That description fits because badgers *love* to dig. Their extra-long front claws and strong forelegs are designed for tunnelling into the earth. Two large back feet allow them to kick the dirt away. Their eyes have a special clear covering that protects them from flying dirt.

But don't be fooled by the badger's baggy skin and its slow, awkward movements. If an animal attacks, the badger's loose skin protects it from getting too badly hurt. With its sharp teeth and nails, this animal can defend itself against just about any attacker. Even larger animals, like coyotes, learn that the badger never backs down in a fight.

Badgers are also fierce hunters. They find ground squirrels and other prey by scent. They dig up their prey's burrows with their powerful claws and attack. If the animal is not there, badgers will sometimes dig out the back of a burrow and crawl in. Then they lie in wait near the entrance.

Imagine you are a ground squirrel. You're heading back to the safety of your burrow for a good long snooze. As you jump head first down the hole, you come face to face with a set of razor-sharp teeth!

Badger strikes again!

CHAPTER FOUR

Burrowing Owl

A burrowing owl could really be called a *borrowing* owl because it often "borrows" the abandoned home of a ground squirrel or badger for its nest.

It may seem strange that an owl would nest underground. But think about it — there aren't many trees or high perches on the prairies, are there? Living in burrows gives this bird a lot more choice in homes.

Burrowing owls have found other ways to adapt to their environment. For example, they have long, stilt-like legs that help them see over short prairie grasses. And while most owls eat only rodents, burrowing owls also dine on insects — a handy food source when you live underground.

Burrowing owls are small — about the size of a robin. Their small size allows them to fit easily inside the ready-made burrows of other animals.

When a pair of owls finds a burrow they like, they use their wings, beaks and feet to make it bigger. Then they plaster the walls with feathers, leaves and dung.

Scientists aren't sure why they do this. It could be to attract dung beetles. YUM! Or perhaps it helps to hide their scent from predators. It could be to strengthen the walls to keep them from collapsing.

Or maybe it makes the burrow warmer so their eggs hatch sooner.

After the babies
are born, they stay
safely underground
for the first two weeks.
As the chicks grow,
the nest gets very
crowded. So the family
often takes over nearby
burrows as well.

If a badger or other predator tries to come
down the hole, the young birds make a
hissing noise. If they're lucky, their attacker
will be fooled into thinking there is a snake
inside the burrow!

Actually, burrowing owls can make at least
17 different noises — from WHO-WHO to
clucks, coos and chucking sounds. What are
they saying? Who-who knows!

CHAPTER FIVE

Coyote

At first glance, coyotes look a lot like their dog cousins. But as soon as they open their mouths, you can tell the difference. Coyotes have very high-pitched voices. They bark, yip, yodel, whine and howl. Sometimes the pups try to imitate their parents. They sound like squeaky violins!

When the pups are born in spring, they are blind and helpless. They stay hidden in a den with their mother. The father protects the den, and also brings food back for his family.

As the pups grow, they become very playful. They like to wrestle, run, chew things and even throw sticks up in the air.

Once they are grown, coyotes are very smart. They can adapt to just about any situation. For example, they use different hunting methods to catch different kinds of prey. For small creatures such as mice, they hunt alone, using their sense of smell. When they find a mouse, they pounce on it!

Other times, they hunt in pairs. One coyote chases the animal toward its partner. The other coyote hides and waits for its meal to arrive. Then the partners change roles.

Sometimes a coyote follows a badger around. When the badger starts digging into a burrow, the coyote waits at another entrance hole and grabs whatever animal tries to escape. What do you think the badger thinks of this arrangement?

CHAPTER SIX

Northern Prairie Skink

Did you know that there is a desert on the prairies? Thousands of years ago, the Carberry Sandhills area in Manitoba was the shore of a giant lake. When the lake dried up, it left behind an area of rolling sand dunes.

Many unique plants and animals live in this region. The northern prairie skink is one of them. In fact, you won't find these interesting reptiles anywhere else in Canada.

Skinks are small lizards about as long as your hand. They spend most of their lives hiding under tree trunks, in shallow burrows or even under pieces of cardboard that have been left lying around.

If you were a skink, your list of favourite meals would include crickets, grasshoppers, spiders, other insects and their *larvae* (LARV-eye) and eggs. Way down at the bottom of the list are ants. Although ants are plentiful, skinks just hate to eat them! No one really knows why, and the skinks aren't talking!

Skinks can be quite colourful. Young ones are easy to spot because of their long, bright blue tails. As they get older, the blue fades.

During the mating season, males develop brilliant orange throat patches. The colour helps them to attract females.

Of course, being so colourful could also attract some unwanted attention from predators. Hognose snakes, hawks, owls, raccoons and mice all eat skinks.

But skinks have a clever way to defend themselves. If an animal or person grabs a skink's long tail, the tail simply falls off. The tail may even shake and jump about on its own for up to 15 minutes! The hunter is usually so surprised, the skink has time to skitter away to safety. And yes, the tail will grow back, but it will be shorter than before.

CHAPTER SEVEN

Red Fox

The first thing you need to know about red foxes is that they are not always red. Some are dark brown or black, with cross-shaped markings on their backs. Some are black with white tips. Still others are silver. Even the red coats can come in many shades, from light to dark. Often pups within the same litter can have all these different colours and markings.

In stories, foxes are usually very clever, very tricky and not to be trusted. In real life, foxes are actually shy, nervous creatures that try to stay hidden as much as possible.

But the stories are right about one thing — foxes really are clever. For example, some foxes have learned to catch fish by leaping into the water on top of a school of lake trout!

Foxes are in the same family as dogs, wolves and coyotes. But being in the same family doesn't mean they are friends. A fox makes a nice meal for a coyote. And in traditional fox hunts, hunters use dogs to find the fox and chase it into the open.

Like their larger cousins, foxes use their sensitive noses to sniff out eggs or other food. They can see the smallest movement from a great distance. Their keen hearing helps them find animals and insects — even the ones that hide underground.

Fox mates usually stay together for life. The mother fox, called a vixen, cares for her young kits in a den that is often a carved-out woodchuck burrow. The father, or dog, brings food back to the den for the mother and cubs.

After a few weeks, both parents will go out hunting and bring back live mice, voles and other small creatures. The cubs learn to hunt by playing with their supper. They let the creature go, then pounce on it and . . . GULP!

CHAPTER EIGHT

Pronghorn

You may have heard some people call the pronghorn an antelope. But that's a mistake. Pronghorns are not closely related to the antelope family. In fact, no other animal on Earth is quite like a pronghorn. Some animals, such as deer and caribou, have long antlers that fall off every year and then grow back. Goats and sheep have shorter horns that never fall off.

Pronghorns have short permanent horns, like goats do. But male pronghorns grow extensions on these horns, which they shed every fall like antlers. Their horns branch off in two directions. Each branch has a small curved spike, or prong, that sticks out toward the front. And that's where the name pronghorn comes from!

Here's something else that makes the pronghorn unique. It is the fastest land animal in North America. In fact, it's one of the fastest animals in the world. At top speed, the pronghorn can go almost 100 kilometres an hour — about as fast as a car on a highway!

A few animals, such as cheetahs, are faster over short distances. But pronghorns can keep up the pace for much longer.

How do you stop the fastest land animal in North America? Actually, it's pretty easy. You put up a fence. Nobody really knows why, but pronghorns will not jump over fences. They prefer to crawl underneath or slip through a crack — if they can.

So when settlers started fencing in the wide open grasslands of the prairies, the pronghorns could not move around. They were stuck, which made it easier for predators to hunt them. So the pronghorn population went down.

Pronghorns are very playful and curious. They sometimes race alongside cars, then run ahead and cross the road in front of the astonished driver!

A pronghorn will often come quite close to check out an unusual object or activity. But when it senses danger, it raises the white hairs on its rear end to warn other pronghorns. The raised white hairs look a bit like a flower blooming!

CHAPTER NINE

Red-Tailed Hawk

High over a field of wheat, a red-tailed hawk swings in long, lazy circles. It barely beats its wings as it rides on the rising currents of air.

Without warning, the hawk suddenly swoops down. As it approaches the ground, it holds its legs out and picks up a tiny field mouse. Then it glides effortlessly upward again to the top of a nearby telephone pole to eat its catch.

Hawks have excellent eyesight. From high in the air, they can spot tiny creatures running through the undergrowth.
The sharp claws on their feet, called talons, allow them to grasp animals as they swoop down on them. And their hooked beak helps them to tear into their prey.

One thing a hawk doesn't have, though, is teeth. It can't chew its food. So it gobbles it down in chunks. The parts that it can't digest — such as fur and bones — are stored in an area of the hawk's throat called the *crop*. In the crop, the material forms into a small round ball, or *pellet*, which the hawk coughs up.

You can tell exactly what animals a hawk has eaten by looking at the bones in its pellets. A red-tailed hawk eats mostly mice, squirrels and other small animals. But sometimes it can attack larger beasts, such as raccoons, porcupines, weasels, cats and even skunks! The red-tail is one of the only creatures that is not bothered by the skunk's smell.

Red-tailed hawks build their nests high up in trees. They prefer to nest in wooded areas that are close to open fields, for easy hunting. Their nests are about a metre wide and can be almost a metre deep. A pair of red-tails often returns to the same nest year after year — unless it is taken over by great horned owls.

Hawk parents make sure that there is always a twig of fresh green leaves in the nest. Scientists are not sure why. Perhaps the greenery helps to hide the chicks and gives them some extra shelter from the sun. Or perhaps this is the hawk's idea of home decorating!

CHAPTER TEN

Bison

A distant rumble. Then the grass rustles. The ground starts to shake. A cloud of grey dust rises. The rumble grows to a MIGHTY ROAR. And suddenly there they are — a huge, moving sea of charging bison!

STAMPEDE!

You probably won't ever see a huge herd of stampeding bison on the prairies today. There are only a few small herds left. But about 300 years ago, tens of millions of bison roamed the open grasslands. If they were alarmed, sometimes they would start to run. Once the stampede began, no one could stop it!

From the front, a bison looks like it belongs in the ice age. At two metres tall, it is one of the largest land animals in North America. Shaggy, matted hair hangs from its head, face, shoulders and forelegs. A hump in its shoulders keeps its head hanging low near the ground.

Two horns grow from the sides of its head. Its nostrils are huge and black, and its tongue is blue.

Sounds scary, doesn't it? But bison are peaceful creatures that want to be left alone to chew grass.

Another favourite activity of bison is wallowing — taking a bath in dirt! It's quite a sight to see such huge beasts wriggling around on their backs to cover themselves in the dust. Once you know the reason for this odd behaviour, though, it makes more sense. Like us, bison are bothered by flies and other insects. The dust keeps the itching down.

Most female bison give birth to only one calf at a time. Pregnancy lasts for close to ten months, and calves are born in the spring. Once they find their feet, baby bison are playful creatures. They like to run and buck alongside their mothers.

A newborn calf may weigh up to 20 kilograms. By the time they are four years old, the females, or cows, can weigh 400 kilograms. But male bison, or bulls, keep growing slowly their whole lives. Since these animals can live 20 years or more, it's no wonder they get so big!

Canada's prairie animals have had to adapt to changes caused by people. But people are learning to adapt too.

For example, farmers used to treat hawks and coyotes as enemies. Today most prairie farmers know that these animals have an important role to play in prairie life. They help to control the mice and rabbits that feed on farm crops.

Up in the air . . .
down on the ground . . .
and underground,
Canada's prairie
animals are awesome!